DATE DUE

Yellow Umbrella Books are published by Capstone Press
151 Good Counsel Drive, P.O. Box 669, Mankato, Minnesota 56002
http://www.capstone-press.com

Library of Congress Cataloging-in-Publication Data
Trumbauer, Lisa, 1963–
    On the go/by Lisa Trumbauer.
    p. cm.
    Includes index.
    ISBN 0-7368-0735-7
    1. Transportation—Juvenile literature. [1. Transportation.] I. Title.
HE152.T76 2001
388—dc21   00-036480

    Summary: Describes the ways people travel, including by car, on foot, by bike, on horses,
on tractors, on buses, on trains, by plane, and by boat.

Editorial Credits:
Susan Evento, Managing Editor/Product Development; Elizabeth Jaffe, Senior Editor;
    Jessica Maldonado, Designer; Kimberly Danger and Heidi Schoof, Photo Researchers

Photo Credits:
Cover: Visuals Unlimited/Jeff Greenberg; Title Page: Unicorn Stock Photos/V.E. Horne; Page 2:
Unicorn Stock Photos/Tommy Dodson; Page 3: Visuals Unlimited/Mark E. Gibson (left),
Stephen Simpson/FPG International LLC (right); Page 4: R. Hamilton Smith (left), Index Stock
Imagery (right); Page 5: Visuals Unlimited/Mark E. Gibson; Page 6: Visuals Unlimited/Inga
Spence; Page 7: Morris Best/Pictor; Page 8: Mark Reinstein/Pictor; Page 9: Gary Buss/FPG
International LLC; Page 10: Photo Network/Mark Sherman (left), Visuals Unlimited/Jeff
Greenberg (right); Page 11: Kent & Donna Dannen; Page 12: Visuals Unlimited/John Sohlden;
Page 13: Visuals Unlimited/D.S. Kerr (left), Unicorn Stock Photos/Frank Pennington (right);
Page 14: Index Stock Imagery; Page 15: International Stock/Mike Agliolo (left), Index Stock
Imagery (right); Page 16: Photo Network/Michael Philip Manheim

1 2 3 4 5 6 06 05 04 03 02 01

ON THE GO

by Lisa Trumbauer

Consulting Editor: Gail Saunders-Smith, Ph.D.
Consultants: Claudine Jellison and
Patricia Williams, Reading Recovery Teachers
Content Consultant: Andrew Gyory, Ph.D., American History

Yellow Umbrella Books

an imprint of Capstone Press
Mankato, Minnesota

People are on the go!
On the go means people
move from place to place.
Some places are near.
Some places are far.

People walking around town
are on the go.
People running in parks
are on the go.

People who skate
and ride bikes are on the go.
They wear helmets to keep
them safe. They have fun
going from place to place
in their neighborhoods.

People who ride horses
are on the go.
People can ride horses
from place to place
on a trail.

People who drive tractors
are on the go.
Farmers use tractors to pull
farm machines from place
to place in their fields.

People who ride in cars
are on the go.
People ride in cars
around town and far away.

People who ride on buses
are on the go.
Many people ride buses
around town or far away.

Some children take buses
to and from school.
You are on the go
when you ride the school bus.

People who ride in trucks
are on the go.
They use trucks to carry
and deliver goods
around town or far away.

People who ride in motor
homes are on the go.
They like to ride to faraway
places in motor homes.

People who ride in trains
are on the go.
Some people ride trains
to get to work, and
some people ride trains
to places far away.

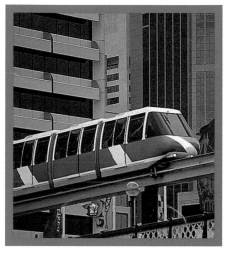

Some trains move
below the ground.
Some trains move
above the ground.

People who ride in boats
are on the go.
They travel from place to
place on oceans, lakes,
and rivers.

People who ride in planes
are on the go.
They fly high in the sky.
People ride planes
to faraway places,
even around the world.

Some people even take
a space shuttle into space!

When you are on the go,
how do you get
from place to place?

Words to Know/Index

Word Count: 311
Early-Intervention Levels: 9–12